Let's discover numbers

PaRragon

Bath · New York · Singapore · Hong Kong · Cologne · Delhi
Melbourne · Amsterdam · Johannesburg · Auckland · Shenzhen

Helping your trainee on their learning adventure

- Choose a time when your child is relaxed and make sure he or she has your full attention. Remember that the activities in this book are to be enjoyed.

- Provide your child with a variety of writing instruments, such as colourful pencils, crayons, pens and markers. Make sure your workspace is organised and well lit.

- Your child does not need to complete each page in one go. Always stop before your child grows tired and come back to the same page another time.

- Always give your child lots of encouragement and praise. Work together so they understand the directions with the option of solo learning if he or she prefers.

- The answers to the activities are on page 47.

First published by Parragon in 2011

Parragon
Queen Street House
4 Queen Street
Bath BA1 1HE, UK

www.chuggington.com
© Ludorum plc 2011

ISBN 978-1-4075-9992-2

Printed in China

Contents

1 chugger.

One

Hold up 1 finger and
say the number 1.

Point to the box that has 1 clock tower.

Practise writing the number 1. Put your pen on the signal
light and follow the arrows along the track.
Then practise writing the number 1 by yourself.

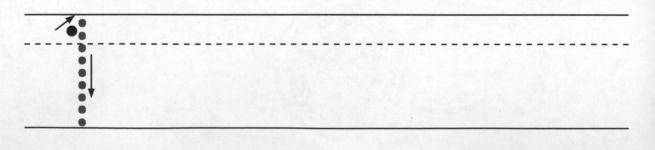

Promote familiarity with a number by asking your
trainee to go over the number with a finger, saying
the number, then trying with their eyes shut.

Count how many chuggers are in each picture
and write the number in the box.

Wilson has lost 1 letter during the mail run. Help Wilson find 1
lost letter by guiding him through the maze.

1 chugger and 1 more chugger
makes **2 chuggers**.

Two

Hold up 2
fingers and
say the number 2.

Point to the box that has 2 horns.

Practise writing the number 2. Put your pen on the signal
light and follow the arrows along the track.
Then practise writing the number 2 by yourself.

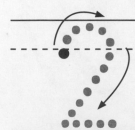

Count how many chuggers are in each picture
and write the number in each box.

Ring the 2 pictures of Brewster and Wilson that are the same.

Play a matching pairs game! Give your trainee an object and
ask them to find another object that matches. Explain that
they now have two of the same.

Odd 1 out

Which picture of Vee is the odd 1 out?
Tick the odd Vee.

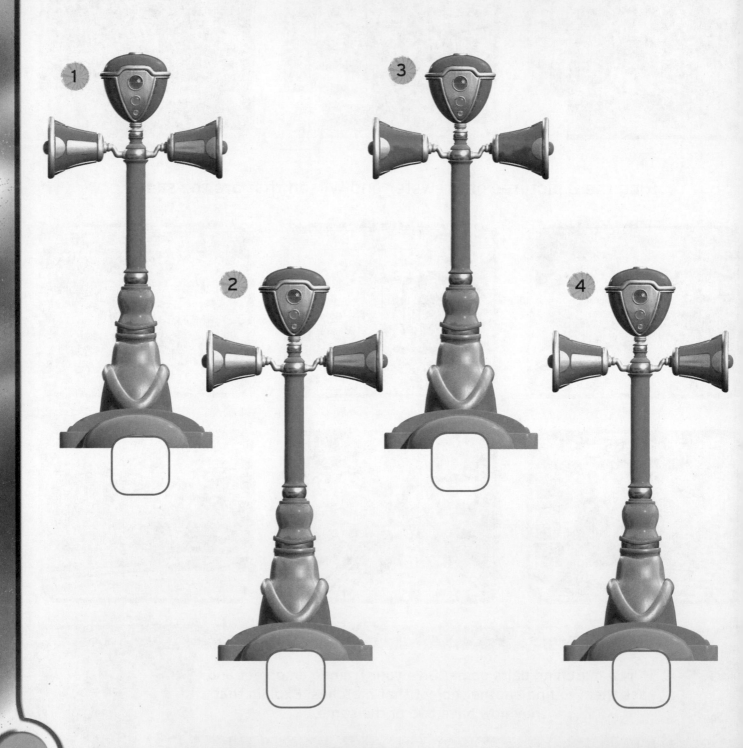

Pairs of 2

When 2 things match, they make a pair. Make animal pairs by drawing lines to connect the matching animals.

Well done!

3 chuggers

2 chuggers and 1 more chugger
makes **3 chuggers**.

Hold up 3 fingers and say the number 3.

Three

Point to the box that has 3 tickets.

Practise writing the number 3. Put your pen on the signal
light and follow the arrows along the track.
Then practise writing the number 3 by yourself.

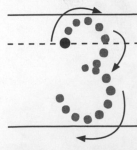

Count how many tunnels are in each picture
and write the answer in the box.

Draw lines to connect the 3 missing pieces to this picture.

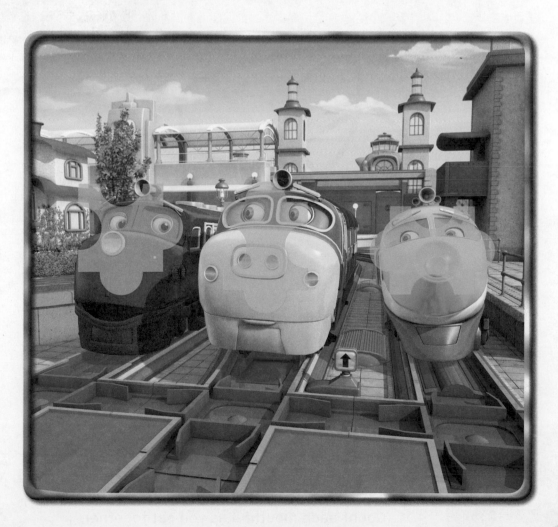

1, 2, 3!

The trainees have lots of jobs to complete, so they are helping each other. Which place will they chugg to first, second and third?

Number 1 shows the first place.
Number 2 shows the second place.
Number 3 shows the third place.

Meal time can help explain the concept of first, second and third to your trainee. Count each mouthful as you eat together.

Let's race!

The trainees have just raced around the depot. Join the different coloured dots together to find out who came first, second and third!

Brewster's number is blue.

Koko's number is purple.

Wilson's number is red.

More or less?

3 is more than 2 and 2 is less than 3. Count the objects below and tick the box which has the most objects.

Count the headlights on each trainee.
Colour in the chugger which has the most headlights.

Count the objects in each box and write the number in the small box.
Draw lines to connect the boxes with the same number.

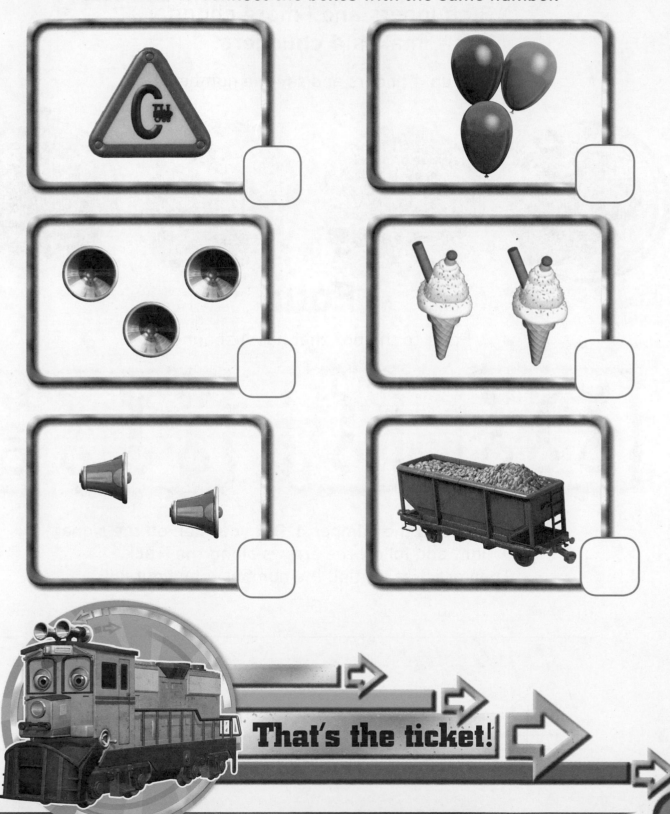

That's the ticket!

3 chuggers and 1 more chugger
makes **4 chuggers**.

Hold up 4 fingers and say the number 4.

Four

Point to the box that has 4 spanners.

Practise writing the number 4. Put your pen on the signal
light and follow the arrows along the track.
Then practise writing the number 4 by yourself.

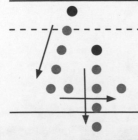

Count how many rivets are in each set and write the answer in the box.

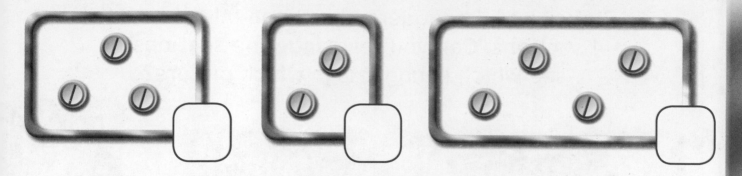

Helpful Hodge is helping Morgan choose paint colours to match his metal work. Ring 4 colours that match Hodge.

Picture mix-up

Pictures of 4 chuggers have been mixed up into 4 sections. Can you rearrange the sections to see which chugger is in which picture?

New moves

The trainees are practising new moves.
Tick move number 4 in each pattern!

A or B

Well done youngster!

5 chuggers

4 chuggers and 1 more chugger
makes **5 chuggers.**

Hold up 5 fingers and say the number 5.

Five

Point to the box that has 5 bumper badges.

Practise writing the number 5. Put your pen on the signal
light and follow the arrows along the track.
Then practise writing the number 5 by yourself.

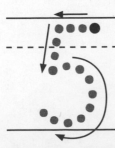

Count how many wheels are in each box and then write the number in the box.

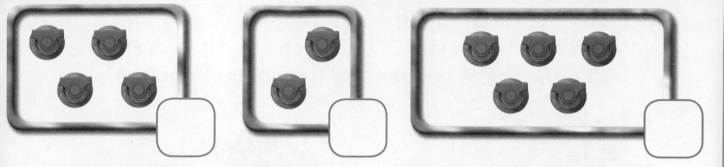

Zephie has spotted 2 friends on the tracks. Can you spot 3 more?

Help your trainee develop the ability to count on by putting two items in front of them and asking them to add more until they have five.

Count up

Each chugger is bringing a different number of balloons to Old Puffer Pete's party. Count each set, then draw lines to connect the balloons to the correct chugger.

1

2

3

4

5

Find 5

Tick the picture that has 5 chuggers.

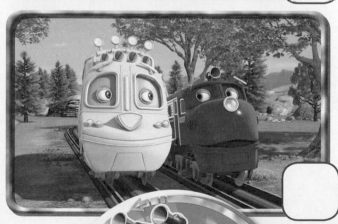

Absotootly amazing!

Missing numbers

Wilson, Koko and Brewster are counting as they chugg.
Fill in the missing numbers so each counts from 1 to 5.

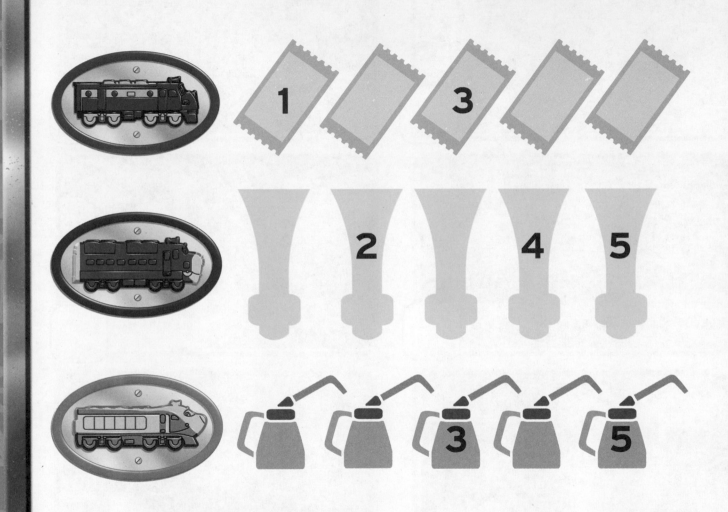

Removing numbers from a line and asking your trainee to
recall the order is a good challenge and stimulates memory.

Can you spot the five differences between these two pictures?
Trace over a number when you find each difference.

1
2
3
4
5

6 chuggers

5 chuggers and 1 more chugger makes **6 chuggers**.

Hold up 6 fingers and say the number 6.

Six

Point to the box that has 6 oil cans.

Practise writing the number 6. Put your pen on the signal light and follow the arrows along the track.
Then practise writing the number 6 by yourself.

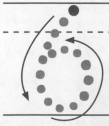

Count how many tickets there are in each set and write the answer in the box.

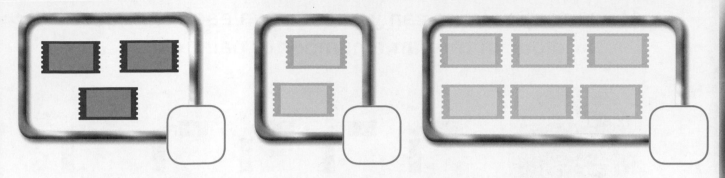

Emery is taking 6 people to the depot. Ring the correct number of tickets he needs to collect.

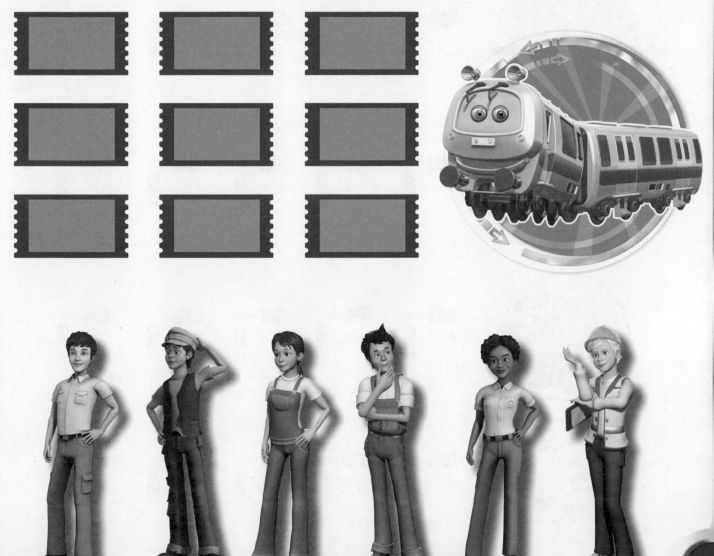

Counting colours

How many colours can you count on each chugger?
Colour in the same number of paint cans.

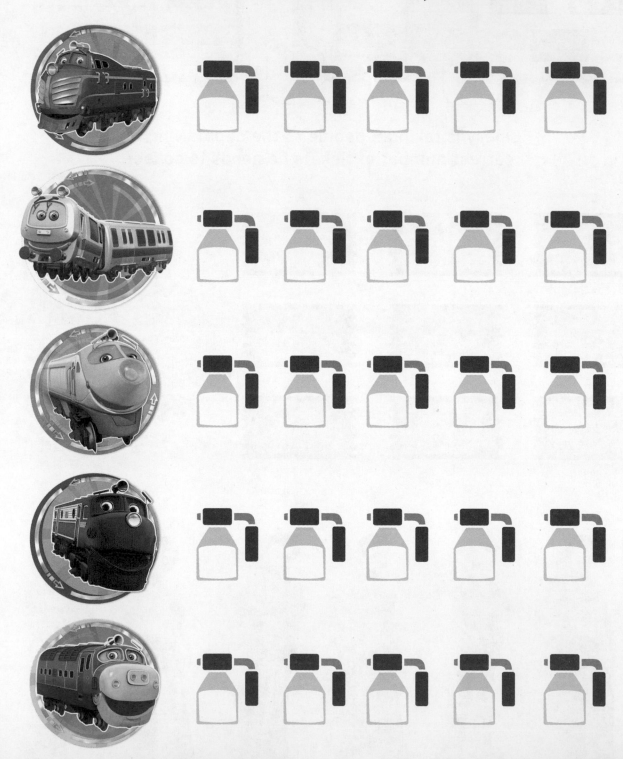

Mtambo's amazing adventure

Guide Mtambo through the Safari Park and count how many of each animal you meet.

Elephants:

Giraffes:

Monkeys:

6 chuggers and 1 more chugger
makes **7 chuggers.**

Hold up 7 fingers and say the number 7.

Seven

Point to the box that has 7 lines of tracks.

Practise writing the number 7. Put your pen on the signal light
and follow the arrows along the track. Then practise
writing the number 7 by yourself.

Tick the box that has 7 signal lights.

Count how many puffs of smoke Old Puffer Pete is puffing.

**7 chuggers and 1 more chugger
makes 8 chuggers.**

Hold up 8 fingers and say the number 8.

Eight

Frostini is making a new flavour of ice cream.
Draw 8 things you would like in an ice cream!

Use the number code to colour in this picture of Frostini.

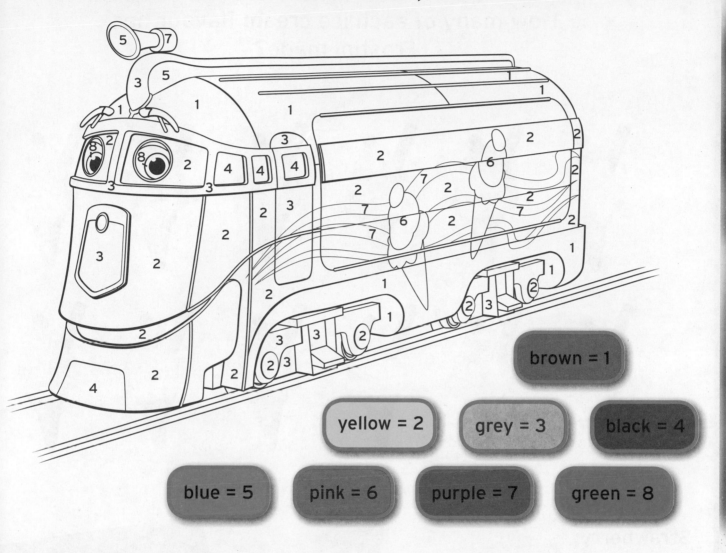

brown = 1

yellow = 2

grey = 3

black = 4

blue = 5

pink = 6

purple = 7

green = 8

Practise writing the number 8. Put your pen on the signal light and follow the arrows along the track. Then practise writing the number 8 by yourself.

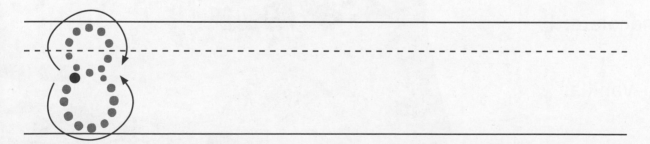

The ice cream factory

How many of each ice cream flavour has Frostini made?

Strawberry: ☐

Mint: ☐

Chocolate: ☐

Vanilla: ☐

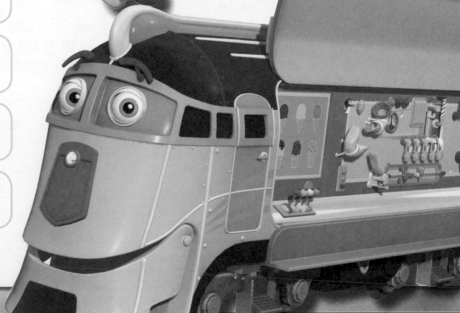

How many pictures is Wilson in? _____

How many pictures is Frostini in? _____

How many pictures are there altogether? _____

Magnifico!

8 chuggers and 1 more chugger
makes **9 chuggers.**

Hold up 9 fingers and say the number 9.

Nine

Tick the box that has 9 oil cans.

The chuggers are racing in the Great Chugger Championship! How many are taking part?

chuggers.

Practise writing the number 9. Put your pen on the signal light and follow the arrows along the track. Then practise writing the number 9 by yourself.

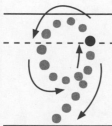

9 chuggers and 1 more chugger
makes **10 chuggers**.

Hold up 10 fingers and say the number 10.

Ten

Find 10 of your favourite things and draw them here.

How many chuggers are red? _____

How many chuggers are green? _____

How many chuggers are there altogether? _____

Practise writing the number 10. Put your pen on the signal light and follow the arrows along the track. Then practise writing the number 10 by yourself.

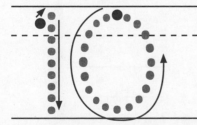

Number picture

Answer 10 traintastic number questions about the depot picture! Wheels to the rails!

1. How many flying chuggers? _____

2. How many squirrels? _____

3. How many chuggers are in the tunnels? _____

4. How many tunnels? _____

5. How many people? _____

6. How many elephants? _____

7. How many lamp posts? _____

8. How many signal lights? _____

9. How many monkeys? _____

10. How many chuggers altogether? _____

Dot to dot

Join the dots 1 to 10 to complete the picture.

Colour in the chuggers!

Trainee-doku

Complete the grids so that each number only appears once in each column and row.

Count and colour

The chuggers are ready for their jobs. How many do you count? Colour a number when you count each chugger.

1

2

3

4

5

6

7 8 9 10

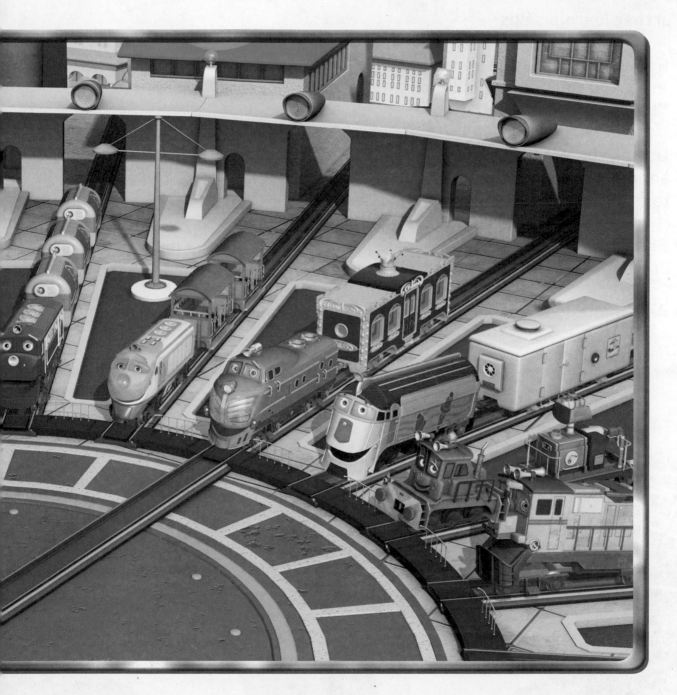

More training time!

Further learning tips:

• Repeating the names of numbers and associating them with objects in a child's environment helps them learn 1-10. For example, "Here are three pens."

• Use all the senses to teach numbers. You can look for numbers on shopping trips, you can touch a different number of toys. You can taste numbers by counting mouthfuls.

• Encourage number recall by asking your child to make a number track. Draw and cut out 10 chuggers, then hang them up or stick onto a wall.

• Ask your child to count the things they see around them during the day.

Answers

Page 4

Page 5

Page 6

Page 8
Vee 3 is the odd one out

Page 9

Page 10

Page 11

Page 12
1 2 3

Page 13
1 - Koko   3 - Brewster
2 - Wilson

Page 14

Page 15

Page 16

Page 17

Page 18
1 - Chatsworth
2 - Calley
3 - Emery
4 - Puffer Pete

Page 19
1 - A   3 - B
2 - B   4 - B

Page 20

Page 21

Page 22

Page 23

Page 24

Page 25

Page 26
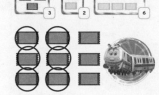

Page 27

Page 28
Harrison - 1 paint can
Emery - 4 paint cans
Koko - 3 paint cans
Wilson - 3 paint cans
Brewster - 2 paint cans

Page 29
3 elephants
4 giraffes
6 monkeys

Page 30

Page 31
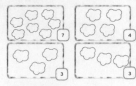

Page 33

Page 34
Strawberry: 5
Mint: 2
Chocolate: 2
Vanilla: 3

Page 35
6 pictures show Wilson
5 pictures show Frostini
6 pictures altogether

Page 36

Page 37
9 chuggers

Page 39
4 chuggers are red
4 chuggers are green
10 chuggers altogether

Pages 40-41
1 - 1   6 - 1
2 - 2   7 - 2
3 - 1   8 - 8
4 - 4   9 - 9
5 - 5   10 - 10

Page 43

Complete your Chuggington collection.
Tick them off as you collect!

stories

  ISBN 978-1-4075-6041-0
 ISBN 978-1-4075-6042-7
 ISBN 978-1-4075-8009-8
 ISBN 978-1-4075-8010-4
 ISBN 978-1-4075-9530-6
 ISBN 978-1-4075-9531-3
 ISBN 978-1-4075-9937-3
 ISBN 978-1-4075-9938-0

CLUNKY WILSON | CAN'T CATCH KOKO | BRAKING BREWSTER | WILSON | KOKO AND THE TUNNEL | BREWSTER GOES BANANAS | PUFFER PETE'S BIG PARADE | JETPACK WILSON

Mini stories

 Braking Brewster — ISBN 978-1-4075-9331-9
 Clunky Wilson — ISBN 978-1-4075-9332-6
 Hodge and the Magnet — ISBN 978-1-4075-9333-3
 Koko and the Squirrels — ISBN 978-1-4075-9334-0
 Wilson Gets a Wash — ISBN 978-1-4075-9335-7
 Zephie's Zoomaround — ISBN 978-1-4075-9336-4

Activity books

 COPY COLOUR POSTER BOOK — ISBN 978-1-4075-6126-4
 STICKER SCENE STORY — 45 STICKERS 6 FANTASTIC SCENES — ISBN 978-1-4075-6044-1
 Bumper Sticker Book — OVER 100 STICKERS INSIDE! — ISBN 978-1-4075-8141-5
 POSTER BOOK — GIANT PULL-OUT POSTER — ISBN 978-1-4075-9529-0
 ACTIVITY BOOK — WITH 6 CHUGGER PUZZLES — ISBN 978-1-4075-9422-4

Little library

 MY FIRST LITTLE LIBRARY — ISBN 978-1-4075-6043-4

Multi-play books

 Construct and Play! — ISBN 978-1-4075-9882-6
 MEET THE CHUGGERS — ISBN 978-1-4075-9884-0

Annual

 CHUGGINGTON ANNUAL 2011 — LET'S RIDE THE RAILS! — ISBN 978-1-84535-437-4

Activity pack

 CHUGGER TRAVEL PACK — ISBN 978-1-4075-9885-7

3D books

 ISBN 978-1-4075-8349-5
 Chugger Sticker Colouring Pad — ISBN 978-1-4075-9780-5

Play books

 SING AND LEARN — ISBN 978-1-4075-6127-1
 KOKO ON CALL — A NIGHT LIGHT ADVENTURE WITH KOKO — ISBN 978-1-4075-8142-2

Story collection

 Storybook Collection — ISBN 978-1-4075-6046-5

Train books

 WILSON LET'S RIDE THE RAILS! — ISBN 978-1-4075-8138-5
 KOKO CHUGGA CHUGGA CHOO CHOO! — ISBN 978-1-4075-8139-2
 BREWSTER HONKING HORNS! — ISBN 978-1-4075-8140-8
 I'M NUMBER ONE! — ISBN 978-1-4075-9784-3